YOUR KNOWLEDGE HAS VALUE

- We will publish your bachelor's and master's thesis, essays and papers

- Your own eBook and book - sold worldwide in all relevant shops

- Earn money with each sale

Upload your text at www.GRIN.com
and publish for free

Bibliographic information published by the German National Library:

The German National Library lists this publication in the National Bibliography; detailed bibliographic data are available on the Internet at http://dnb.dnb.de .

This book is copyright material and must not be copied, reproduced, transferred, distributed, leased, licensed or publicly performed or used in any way except as specifically permitted in writing by the publishers, as allowed under the terms and conditions under which it was purchased or as strictly permitted by applicable copyright law. Any unauthorized distribution or use of this text may be a direct infringement of the author s and publisher s rights and those responsible may be liable in law accordingly.

Imprint:

Copyright © 2017 GRIN Verlag, Open Publishing GmbH
Print and binding: Books on Demand GmbH, Norderstedt Germany
ISBN: 9783668614253

This book at GRIN:

https://www.grin.com/document/387311

Kaia Smith

The role of social norms in legitimating racial inequalities in earnings in the United States

GRIN Publishing

GRIN - Your knowledge has value

Since its foundation in 1998, GRIN has specialized in publishing academic texts by students, college teachers and other academics as e-book and printed book. The website www.grin.com is an ideal platform for presenting term papers, final papers, scientific essays, dissertations and specialist books.

Visit us on the internet:

http://www.grin.com/

http://www.facebook.com/grincom

http://www.twitter.com/grin_com

The role of social norms in legitimating racial inequalities in earnings in the United States

Essay submitted to the International Inequalities Institute, London School of Economics

3 May 2017

Introduction

70% of African-Americans consider racial discrimination a major barrier to their 'getting ahead.' At the same time, only 36% of whites in the US agree that financial success does not take place on a level playing field (Pew Research Center 2016). In a country where blacks are consistently more likely to be poor than whites, there is a seemingly endless list of political, economic, and social reasons for the increasing concentration of poverty within black communities (Jargowsky 2015). For example, blacks continuously face higher unemployment rates than whites and are concentrated in increasingly segregated and low-quality schools (Rothstein 2014). While it is important to analyze such material factors contributing to racial inequalities, it seems important to examine further the phenomenon of polarized beliefs about race and how they may function in the background to contribute to persistent racial income gaps. The purpose of this paper, then, is to make a case for the pertinence of social norms in understanding systematic inequalities in earnings, specifically by looking at norms of racial exclusion and optimism regarding equal social mobility in the US.

Despite an increasing awareness of income inequality in the US, it continues to widen, in part due to lack of effective redistributive policy. These policies are largely shaped by public opinion, and so it seems necessary to look at underlying patterns of social beliefs and preferences. As Sunstein (1996) says, "lives are shortened and unjustified inequalities are perpetuated by the existence of many current norms" (968). In the US in particular, wage inequality has been rising since the 1980s (Goldin & Katz 2007), and most Americans agree that the government should do something to reduce the gap (Pew Research Center 2014). Despite widening income inequality, however, public support for redistribution has stagnated (Ashok, Kuziemko, & Washington 2015). I argue that alongside other material factors, social norms of racial exclusion and optimism about equal access to social mobility in the US have sown an environment in which public support for redistribution, as a remedy for income inequality, remains low. I then discuss feasible norm-centered policies to promote social justice and cohesion.

Theoretical & Empirical Foundations

Income inequality in the US has been increasing steadily since the 1980s. Most pertinently, it maps a divide between black and white segments of the population. With the latter earning 70% more than the former, the economic gap between them is on a near-30-year high. (Wilson & Rogers 2016). Two main paradigms in the social sciences, liberalism and Marxism, are inadequate in accounting for the complexity of this trend and providing solutions. While liberalism claims to value social contracts and equality, this is only to an extent, and even one of its most socially generous representatives, Rawls, accepts inequalities and discrimination as long as the worst-off are adequately benefiting (1971);

additionally, its focus on individual liberties underestimates the value of social freedoms and collective cooperation. Marxism, while accounting for these two things, overemphasizes material factors in the reproduction of inequality; as Marx said, "it is not the consciousness of men that determines their existence, but their social existence that determines their consciousness" (1970). This paper, however, is premised on the mutually constructive relationship between material reality and beliefs, and seeks to emphasize the side overlooked by Marx: consciousness determining social existence in return.

In analyzing public opinion on welfare and redistribution, conventional approaches emphasize either a utilitarian/rational-choice perspective (decisions are based on individual cost-benefit analyses) or a sociological perspective (decisions are primarily based on the structure of social contexts), following Kangas's (1997) classification. Synthesizing these two perspectives, I contend that people are simultaneously self-interested and social, and that each aspect may become more or less salient depending on the context. I focus on the salience of social norms to collective choice in shaping policy on social cohesion, such as welfare, while recognizing that norms may become latent if choices are more relevant to self-interest.

I define social norms broadly as community-based behavioral guidelines, which motivate people to act in certain ways (Durkheim 1950). I borrow from Bicchieri's assertion that, at an individual-cognitive level, norms are based on two types of beliefs: empirical (a critical mass of people obey a certain norm in a similar situation) and normative (a critical mass of people think one should obey the norm in a certain context, and may be willing to sanction a violation). Social norms "typically pertain to situations in which there is an inherent conflict between individual and collective interests" (Bicchieri 2010: 298). Norms can either tax or subsidize choice in that they penalize or reward behavior. They play a formative role in shaping opinions and consequent actions. As such, norms impact policy both directly and indirectly. Political leaders inhabit a normative environment which promises direct behavioral rewards or penalties for policy decisions. And in a democratic context, the public, whose opinions and actions, too, are partial products of norms, has been shown to have substantial bearing on the policymaking process (Risse-Kappen 1991; Sunstein 1996; Brooks & Manza 2007). Sen (1999), in his Capability Approach, elaborates on conversion factors, which determine one's ability to turn a good or service into a capability. Among others, he discusses social conversion factors, including policies and norms, which may pose obstacles to individuals or groups by limiting access to resources or services (Robeyns 2005). For example, systematic racial discrimination within the labor market may limit minorities' access to adequate incomes. In their extensive work on the historical development of within-country income inequality, Piketty (1995) and Atkinson (1997) cite norms as a substantial factor in the persistence and increase in income gaps, alongside economic (e.g. liberalization of markets) and political (e.g. deregulation) explanations (Piketty 1995; Atkinson 1997). Particularly, norms determine the limits of wage differentials, either through outwards shifts of acceptance of inequality within individual workplaces, or exogenous weakening of social norms against inequality after repeated exposure to it (Atkinson 1997). This two-faceted function of norms is supported by empirical evidence of lower public support for redistribution and greater acceptance of wage inequality in more unequal countries (Kerr 2011). Additionally, voters' attitudes towards redistribution are heavily dependent on their economic location and the ideas and policies they are exposed to during their social life at that position (Piketty 1995).

Despite norms being cited as significant barriers to equality by prominent academics studying income inequality, I argue that these references are perfunctory given the impacts that social norms have on shaping opinions and subsequent policies. To illustrate the need for a heightened focus on social norms within this field, I will show how they have impacted on redistribution to African-Americans in the context of persistent racial income inequality.

Norms, Public Opinion, & Policy in the US

Redistribution in the US is consistently lower than in European countries. This asymmetry can only partially be attributed to economic and political factors; norms which instill a sense of optimism in equal social mobility and effect racialized notions of poverty are also important to consider (Alesina, Glaeser, & Sacerdote 2001). Increasingly high levels of income inequality partially stem from low support for redistribution, which is lower among the US public than its European counterparts (Kerr 2011; Alesina et al. 2001) and has stagnated during a period of rising inequality (Ashkok et al. 2015). Americans adhering to this pattern of redistribution aversion (especially conservatives) tend to think that poverty stems from a culture of dependency, rather than structural factors outside of individuals' control (Fong 2001). Moreover, institutional racism is governed by racist norms, and creates inaccurate associations between blacks and inherent disadvantage by discretely or indiscreetly assuming black inferiority, thereby justifying the continuation of racial inequalities (Phillips 2011). Such norms have abetted and justified pejorative associations between African-Americans and poverty, and are largely due to lack of direct interaction and shared experiences. For instance, in highly diverse neighborhoods, the lowest levels of trust are found in affluent areas with low interaction among racial groups, whereas trust is much higher in diverse low-income neighborhoods with high intra-group interaction (Sturgis, Brunton-Smith, Read, & Allum 2011). When it comes to social support, redistributive benefits go mainly to minorities, which creates racial divides in conceptions of welfare; and importantly, race is the most important predictor for welfare preferences among individuals (Alesina et al. 2001: 4). Blacks and other minorities are more likely than whites to consider welfare helpful in making it out of poverty, whereas large numbers of conservative whites claim that welfare breeds dependency (Lauter 2016).

An additional explanation for redistributive preferences in the US is the widespread belief that everyone has an equal chance to 'get ahead' and escape poverty, which is not nearly as pervasive in more redistributive countries (Benabou & Tirole 2006). This view not only lends itself to blaming African-Americans for their disadvantaged economic position, but also to downplaying the importance of a social safety net for those in need. Alesina and La Ferrara (2001) show that stronger beliefs in the fairness and accessibility of the mobility process in the US is significantly and negatively associated to support for redistribution. However, half of parental income advantages are passed on intergenerationally, demonstrating that moving up the socioeconomic strata is not as much about hard work as people may think (Mitnik & Grusky 2015). In a study measuring gaps between perceived and actual economic mobility, Americans overestimated upward movement by an average of 23% (Kraus & Tan 2015). Because luck is a large determinant of mobility, this normative optimism seems to be misinformed, and likely premised on systematic ignorance of the detriment of increasing income inequality, including the pronounced disadvantages blacks face relative to whites in 'getting ahead.'

Patterns of racialized aversion to welfare and optimism regarding upward social mobility demonstrate that economic preferences based solely on self-interest cannot account for widespread contradictory stances on inequality and redistribution. Furthermore, political explanations fall short of fully illuminating persistent racial inequality. Elimination of racial discrimination in US law cannot explain continued inequality and exclusion in the face of dominant norms that exist outside the scope of the conventional legal realm (see Lacey 1987). As Brown (2013) posits, "the demise of de jure discrimination has done little to diminish the centrality of race in American politics (…) [and] racial attitudes (…) remain among the most powerful predictors of policy opinions and outcomes" (395). Welfare policy, although formulated with race-neutral language, preserves pre-Civil-Rights-Era patterns of disadvantage. For example, more ethnically fragmented US states spend less on social services and more on crime prevention (Alesina et al. 1999). And the 1996 welfare reforms, influenced by racialized norms on welfare, toughened benefit sanctions for long periods of unemployment without acknowledging difficulties posed by institutional employer racism (Constance-Higgins 2011). The persistence of such norms, therefore, augments material structural limitations on blacks' ability to narrow the income gap.

Generally, norms are fluid, and the relationship between norms and inequality is reflexive. As Austen (1999) writes, "an important dynamic relationship appears to exist between levels of inequality and the normative structures that relate to them. Levels of inequality influence attitudes to inequality, and, thus, changes in inequality are likely to have ongoing effects on the wage structure" (442). Therefore, norms depend on micro-level social experiences as well as macro-level contextual perceptions of individuals. Bicchieri (2010) shows empirically that adherence to social norms is flexible, and policies which endorse inclusive norms should attempt to change expectations about how others behave and how others think one should behave in similar situations. Therefore, recognition of the compounded disadvantages which facilitate the black-white income gap is needed to highlight the inaccuracies that racist norms perpetuate and reduce their legitimacy and adherence. Approaches to reducing income inequalities should seek to update social norms by addressing the dissonance between a collective desire for social justice and empirical reality as well as increasing direct interaction between groups.

Policy Prescriptions

Because norms can be communicated to the public as appropriate by macro-level contexts and organizations, political institutions themselves can promote norms of equality. Across OECD countries, higher income inequality is correlated with lower electoral participation (Lister 2007). And in the US, people receiving means-tested benefits participate less and feel less politically effective than recipients of broader social insurance schemes (Soss 1999). This illustrates that norms not only affect voting behavior, but also who votes and thereby impacts policy. Therefore, governments can enforce norms of solidarity by making institutions more inclusive. In particular, inclusive welfare systems can increase solidarity by redistributing both resources and risk (Lister 2007: 24), thus increasing the likelihood of civic participation by signaling the positive value of collective action and by increasing visibility of others' participation in collective well-being. This could mean switching from means-testing to broader social insurance benefits, for example by providing benefits to middle and lower classes (rather than solely the most disadvantaged) to avoid associations with dependency culture (Wilson 1998). Directly, this would entail higher well-being for welfare recipients, and indirectly, this could contribute to inclusive norm-building as equality in minimum levels of well-being becomes routinized.

Additionally, public spaces should be utilized for integrated civic participation and community-building, for example, free exercise classes or community volunteering projects. This would require both research on how to interest diverse groups and thoughtful planning to spur interaction. Such efforts could help in reaching the perceived critical mass of adherents to norms of inclusiveness. Organizations and the government could collaborate in celebrating diversity in these spaces by holding public events and festivals. They could also disseminate educational material about the dynamics of racial inequalities. In order to achieve social justice, both economic redistribution and a sociocultural recognition of processes of exclusion are necessary (Fraser & Honneth 2003). As the awareness of new facts may change normative behaviors (Sunstein 1996), it is important for political/organizational leaders and the press to identify and publicly discuss inconsistencies in opinions held about inequalities. Specifically, the negative human impacts of income inequality on black communities and the resulting compounded disadvantage require detailed attention, as does the resulting need for inclusive social safety nets. In order to address simplified associations between racial differences and poverty, information about the complexity of racial inequalities and the lasting legacies of institutional racism should be made more accessible.

However, the interpretation of such information may also be influenced by norms themselves. On that account, government can take a more direct role in norm management to increase equality and societal well-being (Sunstein 1996). Policies should target racially exclusionary norms by championing both *de jure* and *de facto* racial equality (e.g. ensure national minimums of benefit coverage to avoid discrepancies in welfare provision between areas of high and low racial divisions). Also, legally binding sanctions against certain exclusionary normative behaviors are conceivable. This approach may not be without controversy: firstly, the very nature of norms' functioning is that they are more effectively established endogenously than exogenously; and secondly, establishing value judgments for which group's norms are (in)valid could result in antidemocratic prescriptions. Nonetheless, it merits consideration in the face of widespread social norms that legitimate systematic income inequality to the detriment of a minority group.

Conclusion

This paper's normative approach does not presume to autonomously explain the persistence of socioeconomic inequality or to provide a panacea against it. In fact, the impalpability of normative processes and the extent to which they are intermeshed with material conditions renders an isolated analysis difficult, if not undesirable. Emphasizing the importance of norms in legitimating income inequality, specifically between whites and blacks in the US, has therefore rather been a concise attempt at complementing conventional accounts. A more extensive examination of social norms and inequality would be well-advised to include economic, political, and other social explanations and solutions as well. It should also be kept in mind that norm-oriented policy is a difficult undertaking and efforts at norm management may produce backlash when coinciding with low levels of popular support for the government or with competing subcultural norms (Sunstein 1996). In order to further develop a normative approach to inequality, a longitudinal analysis of normative contexts in other countries that tolerate high levels of income inequality as well as an examination of ethical methods of norm management for the purposes of equality and social justice are encouraged.

In this paper, I have emphasized the importance of a normative approach to reducing income inequalities through the lens of racialized norms relating to welfare and mobility in the US. Social norms are highly complex, and especially hard to define and measure; perhaps this is part of why they are not as established in the income inequality literature as economic and political explanations. However, in shaping public opinion in segments of the American electorate, norms of pejorative racial associations to poverty and over-optimism regarding equal social mobility have had a significant impact on redistributive policy outcomes. I conclude that norms of racism and optimism regarding equal social mobility in the US have lent legitimacy to sustaining, if not increasing, contemporary racial income inequality both within the public and among policymakers. The persistence of a plethora of racial inequalities as evidenced by the income gap between black and white Americans is hardly random but premised on institutionalized normative patterns of individual preferences and decisions. Consequently, policymaking must account for this structural normative underbelly in order to thoroughly address the detrimental societal outcomes of racial income inequalities. Specifically, the government should cooperate with civil society in educating the public about the dissonance between societal beliefs about inequality and empirical reality, support and promote diversity and inclusive community-building, and perhaps even direct action on normative shifts toward increased equality and social cohesion through legal means. Norm-focused approaches account for the wide discrepancies in awareness of racial barriers to 'getting ahead,'; by opening up the black box of patterns of public opinion, they thereby offer a more thorough perspective from which to effectively address the persistence of inequality. Other countries with such empirical-normative discrepancies in increasing income inequality trends would do well to incorporate such approaches.

References

Alesina, A. & La Ferrara, E. (2001) *Preferences for Redistribution in the Land of Opportunities*. National Bureau of Economic Research, Cambridge, MA.

Alesina, A., Glaeser, E., & Sacerdote, B. (2001) *Why doesn't the US have a European-style welfare system? (NBER working paper series),* 8524th edn. National Bureau of Economic Research.

Ashok, V., Kuziemko, I., & Washington, E. (2015) Support for Redistribution in an Age of Rising Inequality: New Stylized Facts and Some Tentative Explanations. *Brookings Papers on Economic Activity*, 367–405.

Atkinson, A. B. (1997) Bringing Income Distribution in From the Cold. *The Economic Journal* 107 (441), 297–321.

Austen, S. (1999) *Norms of inequality*, Murdoch, WA.

Benabou, R. & Tirole, J. (2006) Belief in a Just World and Redistributive Politics. *Quarterly Journal of Economics* 121 (2), 699–746.

Bicchieri, C. (2010) Norms, preferences, and conditional behavior. *Politics, Philosophy & Economics* 9 (3), 297–313.

Brooks, C. & Manza, J. (2007) *Why Welfare States Persist: The Importance of Public Opinion in Democracies (Studies in Communication, Media, and Public Opinion)*. University Of Chicago Press.

Brown, H. (2013) Racialized Conflict and Policy Spillover Effects: The Role of Race in the Contemporary U.S. Welfare State. *American Journal of Sociology* 119 (2), 394–443.

Durkheim, E. (1950) *Professional Ethics and Civic Morals*. The Free Press, Glencoe, IL.

Fong, C. (2001) Social preferences, self-interest, and the demand for redistribution. *Journal of Public Economics* 82 (2), 225–246.

Fraser, N. & Honneth, A. (2003) *Redistribution or recognition?: A political-philosophical exchange*. Verso, London.

Goldin, C.D. & Katz, L.F. (2007) *Long-run changes in the U.S. wage structure: Narrowing, widening, polarizing*. National Bureau of Economic Research, Cambridge, MA.

Jargowsky, P. (2015) Architecture of Segregation: Civil Unrest, the Concentration of Poverty, and Public Policy. *The Century Foundation*.

Kangas, O. E. (1997) Self-interest and the common good: The impact of norms, selfishness and context in social policy opinions. *The Journal of Socio-Economics* 26 (5), 475–494.

Kerr, W. R. (2011) *Income inequality and social preferences for redistribution and compensation differentials*. National Bureau of Economic Research, Cambridge, MA.

Kraus, M.W. & Tan, J.J.X. (2015) Americans overestimate social class mobility. *Journal of Experimental Social Psychology* 58, 101–111.

Lacey, N. (1987) Legislation against sex discrimination: Questions from a feminist perspective. *Journal of Law and Society* 14 (4), 411–421.

Lauter, D. (2016) How do Americans view poverty?: Many blue-collar whites, key to Trump, criticize poor people as lazy and content to stay on welfare. *LA Times: The Poverty Project*.

Lister, M. (2007) Institutions, Inequality and Social Norms: Explaining Variations in Participation. *The British Journal of Politics and International Relations* 9 (1), 20–35.

Marx, K. (1970) *Contribution to the critique of political economy*. Progress Publishers, Moscow.

Mitnik, P. & Grusky, D. (2015) *Economic Mobility in the United States*.

Pew Research Center (2016) *On Views of Race and Inequality, Blacks and Whites Are Worlds Apart*. http://www.pewsocialtrends.org/2016/06/27/on-views-of-race-and-inequality-blacks-and-whites-are-worlds-apart/

Pew Research Center (2014) *Most See Inequality Growing but Partisans Differ Over Solutions*. http://www.people-press.org/2014/01/23/most-see-inequality-growing-but-partisans-differ-over-solutions/.

Phillips, C. (2011) Institutional Racism and Ethnic Inequalities: An Expanded Multilevel Framework. *Journal of Social Policy* 40 (1), 173–192.

Piketty, T. (1995) Social Mobility and Redistributive Politics. *The Quarterly Journal of Economics* 110 (3), 551–584.

Rawls, J. (1971) *A Theory of Justice*. Belknap Press of Harvard University Press, Cambridge, MA.

Reckwitz, A. (2002) Toward a Theory of Social Practices: A Development in Culturalist Theorizing. *European Journal of Social Theory* 5 (2), 243–263.

Risse-Kappen, T. (1991) Public opinion, domestic structure, and foreign policy in liberal democracies. *World politics* 43 (4), 479-512.

Robeyns, I. (2005) The Capability Approach: A Theoretical Survey. *Journal of Human Development* 6 (1), 93–117.

Rothstein, B. (1998) *Just Institutions Matter: The Moral and Political Logic of the Universal Welfare State (Theories of Institutional Design)*. Cambridge University Press, Cambridge, UK.

Rothstein, R. (2015) The Racial Achievement Gap, Segregated Schools, and Segregated Neighborhoods: A Constitutional Insult. *Race and Social Problems* 7 (1), 21–30.

Sen, A. (1999) *Development as Freedom*. Oxford University Press, New York.

Soss, J. (1999) Lessons of Welfare: Policy Design, Political Learning, and Political Action. *American Political Science Review* 93 (2), 363–380.

Sturgis, P., Brunton-Smith, I., Read, S., & Allum, N. (2011) Does Ethnic Diversity Erode Trust?: Putnam's 'Hunkering Down' Thesis Reconsidered. *British Journal of Political Science* 41 (01), 57–82.

Sunstein, C. R. (1996) Social Norms and Social Roles. *Columbia Law Review* 96 (4), 903.

Wilson, W. J. (1998) *When work disappears: New implications for race and urban poverty in the global economy*. Centre for Analysis of Social Exclusion, London School of Economics, London.

Wilson, V. & Rodgers, W.M. (2016) Black-white wage gaps expand with rising wage inequality. *Economic Policy Institute*. http://www.epi.org/publication/black-white-wage-gaps-expand-with-rising-wage-inequality

YOUR KNOWLEDGE HAS VALUE

- We will publish your bachelor's and master's thesis, essays and papers

- Your own eBook and book - sold worldwide in all relevant shops

- Earn money with each sale

Upload your text at www.GRIN.com
and publish for free